The Modern Historian

The US Financial Crisis of 2008

A Quick Reference Guide

By D.M. Alon

Copyright information

Alon, Doron.

The Modern Historian: The US Financial Crisis of 2008 - A Quick Reference Guide –1st ed

Printed in **The United States**

ISBN: 978-0692590164

Images used for Cover and content:

Cover Created by Doron Alon

Cover image:Wall Street (Image is in the public domain)

http://pl.wikipedia.org/wiki/Wall_Street#mediaviewer/File:Wall -Street.jpg

Introduction

This most recent financial crisis of 2008 was by far one of the scariest economic disasters ever witnessed in modern times. I worked on Wall Street throughout the mid to late 90s and early 2000s as a commodities trader and broker and investor. I thought I witnessed markets at their bloodiest, at least on a professional level. Asia's property bubble burst into a billion pieces; Russia Defaults on its debts, The LTCM bailout and the tech sector imploded under its own weight. All 4 resulting in substantial casualties. I saw various different markets crash and then rise hundreds of points in a matter of seconds and then crash once again. Panic turned into elation only to plummet into a deep sustained panic. Everyone wanted out; it was a pretty scary time. Wall Street was no longer paved with gold, but was running slick with blood.

Suffice it to say, I left that life behind in early 2000 as the crisis was getting worse. I vowed never to return. But I did. In the summer of 2007, I worked as a contractor for Merrill Lynch, mainly in compliance. It was at Merrill when I recalled one of the first signs of things to come. I will be covering some of the major signs in this book.

One of the most ominous signs was Bear Stearns announcement that it would halt redemptions of two of its funds that invested heavily in mortgages. It was big news, but little did most people know that the roof was about to collapse and a huge financial black hole would swallow whatever was left. Like most black holes, they are hard to detect, it's only after they start swallowing up neighboring stars that we know that they exist at all.

The financial crisis was no doubt a recession and some would say a depression; everyone wants to sugar- coat it. Academics want to nitpick and perform magic tricks with the numbers and say it was only a recession. The reality is, no one has seen this before. It was clear, the game has changed. The old definition of what a recession was is no longer sufficient to express what happened. But yet, nothing has really changed. Proof of this can be seen in how the financial world has handled the crisis. The same old theories from the ivory tower are still in place. But for the first time, in a major way, the theories aren't working anymore and people are noticing. The Black hole is still there and money is being thrown into it. A black hole gets larger as it is filled. It's not over, not by a long shot.

In this book, we will cover, ever so briefly, the financial crisis of 2008.

The Chicken or the Egg?

Like most events in financial history, it is not always clear what causes a financial crisis. Aside from obvious signs of strain, there is always a debate as to what truly happens prior to an economic downturn. The Great Depression of the early 20th century is no exception. The most popular answer as to what caused the great depression is the collapse of the stock market in 1929. On the surface, this seems plausible. Immediately after the crash, the economy tanked and banks were failing left and right. This crash was so impactful on the psyche of the populace that all sorts of myths surrounded it. But, like any major event, it's far more complicated. Often a series of smaller events need to occur before the floor gives way. This is as true in our own time as it has been throughout human history.

Until this day, there are studies and books being published as to what started the great depression. Since this book is about the current financial crisis, I will just briefly go over some of the more popular ideas of why the great depression occurred since it relates to the 2008 crisis.

As I stated earlier, the popular notion is that the stock market crash was to blame, however, there were a few other factors; major ones. For starters, the demand for credit all but dried up (Sound Familiar?). Credit for better or for worse drives economic output. Without credit, modern society would be doomed. Without credit, buying power shrivels and ultimately trade slows down. When trade slows down, commodity prices as well as other assets will also go down. No money - No demand. This in turn causes companies to close or cut back, leading to massive unemployment. Again...Sound familiar?

The reason above is mostly a Keynesian or demand driven perspective. In the above scenario, a cycle is created, as prices drop people pull out their money thinking they can avoid further drops in prices. This further erodes price and demand.

Another explanation comes from the monetarist school of thought that believes the great depression was due to a contraction in the supply of money by the Federal Reserve. When a contraction occurs, there is less money in the system. This is done by manipulating interest rates. As rates rise, money becomes more expensive and thus, scarce. When rates are low, it's easier to borrow money and more people do, thus causing a monetary expansion. Ben Bernanke who was at the helm of the Federal Reserve during the crisis is a monetarist. If you have been watching the crisis unfold, you will see how monetarist economics work. The raising and lowering of interest rates is monetarist in nature. But that does not mean it doesn't influence demand. It certainly does. So in essence the US economy is a hybrid of monetarist and demand driven economics. When there is lower interest rates, people borrow and buy more. This is what happened during the most recent financial crisis. But things have changed quite a bit.

There are, of course, several other theories as to what happened, but these are the broader theories. It will be interesting to see how things will change with Janet Yellen, who is a Keynesian. I suspect things will remain the same. Mostly because there isn't that many tricks they can pull out of the bag at this point

In reality, Monetarist theory and Keynesian theory are both two sides of the same coin. Both sides are a form of government planning. They have both coalesced and incorporate a free market ideology. An ideology in which government is not to interfere with supply and demand but rather let market forces dictate prices. It's ironic that the United States considers itself a free market economy while the Federal Reserve tinkers with interest rates which is a form of control. The Federal Reserve policies do not require the president's approval or any other body of the government; although its existence is due to US government statutes. In the next chapter we will discuss the idea of the free market as it applies to our modern predicament.

The Free Market Love Fest

As the 80s rolled in, Ronald Reagan became president of the United States. When he took office in 1981, things were looking grim for the economy. The United States suffered horrible stagnation in the 70s and it wasn't looking good at all. Inflation was through the roof and interest rates were very close to 20%. America was stagnating and slowly losing its edge. Many believed that part of the stagnation was due to over regulation of the markets and financial institutions. With Ronald Reagan at the helm, things were about to change.

Enter Reaganomics.

Reaganomics ushered in a new age of prosperity for the United States as a whole and much of it is still in place to this day. The main pillars of Reaganomics are:

Reducing Income Tax on the federal level.

Reduction in Capital Gains Taxes.

Curtailing Government Spending.

Controlling the money supply through the manipulation of interest rates.

Last but not least:

Reduce government regulation.

This policy was a boon for business. In 1981, he lifted price controls for petroleum products and lowered the oil windfall profit tax which was implemented by the Carter administration to recoup some of the money lost from the OPEC oil embargo of 1973. Eventually, in 1988, he abolished the tax altogether. He essentially continued where Nixon left off in terms of getting rid of price controls of various kinds. In an unpopular move, at least for those making less than $50,000, he lowered taxes on the wealthy and raised it for everyone making under $50,000.

The mixture of deregulation and tax breaks for the wealthy were to pave the way for our current situation. Especially the banking regulatory changes. In 1982, the Garn-St Germain Depository Institutions Act was passed which opened the door for banks to invest in risky real estate assets and risky loans. This led to easing of regulations and few regulatory staff available to monitor the banks. This eventually led to the savings and loan crisis of 1989 which saw bank failures due to risky investments but also fraudulent dealings. Essentially, no one was watching the bankers. But he was not the only one to blame for the banks' risky dealings.

Fast forward to 1999 and we have president Clintons' signing of the Financial Services Modernization Act which allowed Investment banks, insurance companies and banks to merge. Thus repealing a depression era safeguard called the Glass-

Steagall Act. This act was put in place to separate these entities and contain systemic risk to the entire financial system. Now that this act was repealed, any part of a financial firm be it a bank subsidiary or investment bank could make risky investments and write insurance on even riskier investments. If the roof were to fall, it would fall on the entire organization and could not be easily contained to just one unit. This is what we saw during this most recent crisis. Whole firms were damaged not just a subsidiary or a unit. As you can see, deregulation is not truly a partisan issue, both sides of the aisle support deregulation of the financial markets. In essence, this debacle can be blamed on both parties and not just one person, no matter what each party says.

One could ask 'why did they push so hard for deregulation?' The answer is simple, MONEY. These banks and firms lobbied the politicians and as we can see now... Money talks. Everyone or at least most in the United States governing bodies have a price. But to be fair, it may not only be due to greed. There are ethical people out there. But the truth is, in order to get reelected, you need money. Lobbyists are an easy source of cash. If you want to learn more about how lobbying influences politics, I highly recommend the following books: " This Town" By Mark Leibovitch. "The Plutocrats" by Chrystia Freeland and "Winner Take All Politics" by Jacob S. Hack and Paul Pierson .

In the following chapters, we will discuss how free market ideology and interest rate manipulation caused the perfect storm.

As Long As The Music Is Playing...

No one has gotten more flack for ruining the economy than Former head of the Federal Reserve, Alan Greenspan. Ok, maybe George W. Bush...

From 2000 through 2004, Greenspan lowered interest from a high of over 6% to a very low 1% by 2004. From that point onward, the rates would rise slowly. His low interest rate policy was due to several factors. We had a massive tech bubble that burst and the markets were very shaky, and then we had 9-11 and then several accounting scandals. All these events created fear in the markets and the Federal Reserve had to do something. When a crisis occurs, they lower rates so money and credit will be easily obtainable.

The thing is, it was so easy to get credit, that pretty much everyone could get a loan. I recall seeing ads on TV for "no money down loans" or" interest-only loans". I recall telling my friend that this will not end well, but I had no idea at all this would lead to such utter devastation, nor could I see how it would unfold.

At the time, George W. Bush was gung-ho about everyone owning a home. The bankers took this as a sign to lend as much as they could. In the past, people needed to be fairly well qualified to get loans, but now, almost anyone could get a loan.

Even people who had no income. They called those loans "N.I.N.J.A" loans. No Income No Job and Assets. Some lenders were so eager to lend money; some of them did not even have documentation to sign. Just show them anything and they will get you a loan, you can sign later. Often these loans were for 100% or more of the value of the property. Some people would take loans like this and then cross collateralize it with other homes. Some borrowers would have several loans with the same bank on several properties without the income to support them. Often many of the borrowers had bad credit and thus those loans were called "subprime" mortgage loans. With property prices roaring, no one thought that one day they might come back down to earth. Everyone was making money.

Interest rates were so low, banks lent an obscene amount of money and the demand for that money was there. Banks fell over backwards to give you money. Unfortunately for buyers, many of these loans had adjustable rates. This means that the initial low or no rate they received when signing for the loan would disappear at some point in the future and depending on the interest rate climate, the new adjustable rate could be substantially higher, which in turn would increase the mortgage payment by hundreds if not thousands of dollars a month. And you guessed it; as these loans were about to adjust, rates were going up. As the rates went up, demand for new homes dropped. This caused prices to drop and suddenly loans were not only unaffordable, they exceeded the value of the homes they were secured by. The aftermath of unaffordable mortgages led to a massive amount of foreclosures. But this alone wasn't the whole story. If that wasn't bad enough, it was what was happening to these loans behind the scenes that really almost knocked out the economy. (We will discuss that in future chapters.)

As cracks began to appear in the housing markets, banks kept on lending. Citi group's chief at the time, Chuck Prince infamously said "As long as the music is playing, you've got to get up and dance...We're still dancing"

Unfortunately, the music did stop and the dancing eventually turned into a funeral procession for the economy and might I add, his job.

Financial Witchcraft

So the main question is, why would a bank lend money to an unqualified borrower? Don't they know that if they default, the bank would lose? I am pretty sure they did, but as I mentioned in the previous chapter, the risky lending itself was not the full story. The defaults and foreclosures would certainly cause much of the housing collapse, but it was exacerbated several times over by the financial witchcraft that was being performed on these loans. A spell was cast on the banks to lend more money. We will discuss the financial sorcery that was used to make banks lend to everyone who walked in.

In a normal world, Banks generally make money on the loans they write as well as mortgage application fees etc. Although that was part of the lending craze, it was pale in comparison to what those loans were worth to the investment banks and mortgage insurers. Both were paying and receiving big money for those loans.

Here is why.

Investment banks and mortgage buyers like the quasi-governmental agencies; Fannie Mae, Freddie Mac and Ginnie Mae started to buy bank loan portfolios in droves. This was great for the banks, not only did they make money on the initial mortgage application fees; they also made money when the investment banks bought the loans. In addition, another perk was that now the loan itself was no longer the banks responsibility. If the loan defaulted, it wasn't on them anymore. The investment banks effectively bought the loans from normal commercial banks. Then the commercial banks took that money and lent it out all over again making the same fees over and over again. What was really scary is that some banks offered loans to the investment banks to buy the mortgage loans from them. This way, banks had multiple stream of income off their mortgage portfolios. This, of course increased risk as well. This cycle was endless.

The investment banks would then bundle these loans together into products called Mortgage-Backed Securities or MBS. Another term for this kind of repackaging of debt is CDO or collateralized debt obligations. (In this book, ill simply refer to MBS as the investment vehicle for simplicity's sake.) These MBS' were backed by a pool of mortgages. When someone buys an MBS they are buying the income stream from that pool. This could be in the form of interest payments or of principal payments of the underlying loan. MBS can be bought and sold like other investments. Anyone can buy a piece of a larger MBS. Anyone from individual investors to large institutional ones. Investment firms were making a fortune in fees from these purchases and sales. In essence, one loan could be cut up and packaged so that several investors could have a piece of the same loan. Even that piece can be sliced up and repackaged yet again.

Each time it was sliced and diced the banks collected more and more fees.

The fees were so great; the investment banks pushed the lenders to keep the loans coming. Since banks already lent to qualified customers, they needed to make more loans so they could then sell them to the investment banks. So banks tapped into the subprime market. The fees the investment banks made selling, trading and insuring these MBS products was enormous. In fact, Wall Street was once again paved with gold, but this time it was diamond encrusted as well. Wall Street was the richest it has ever been. More millionaires and billionaires were made during this initial glut of MBS and MBS related products than at any other time. There were people making billion dollar paydays. BILLION DOLLAR!

The quasi-governmental agencies; Fannie Mae, Freddie Mac and Ginnie Mae would often guarantee some MBS from default. This was a very attractive feature and people invested through them. An added plus, the government backed some of them in case of a default. It was a no-lose proposition. Or so it seemed.

MBS are complicated instruments. But at the same time, they are very flexible. The investment banks could slice up MBS in many different ways. Banks knew they had a hot investment vehicle with the MBS, so they decided to innovate a bit more with them.

Since loans could be bundled up into type. I.e. Risk level, maturity date, interest rates. They decided to cut up the loans even further into something called "Tranches". For example, let's say the average mortgage in the MBS is 10 years to final payoff. They would slice up the MBS so that they could create a tranche that only represented the first 3 years of payments. This is relatively safe since for the most part, in a normal economy, people don't generally default within the first 3 years. Some investors might take the middle portion of the maturity; let's say 5-8 years of the payments. It's riskier, but the return is greater. So one loan could be spliced up into several tranches. Imagine this on a huge scale.

The greatest risk is that the borrowers would default. If they defaulted, the MBS would take a hit and the investor who bought the MBS would take a loss, that is, if it wasn't guaranteed. Then someone thought, "Lets create an insurance product that would insure against a default". Thus entered, the credit default Swap.

It's All About The Ratings Nowadays.

Blythe Masters, an economist and current chief of Global Commodities for JP Morgan Chase created a brilliant and innovative financial instrument. In 1994, she created something called a credit default swap or CDS. As the name implies, it is an agreement that swaps one thing for another. In a CDS, a seller of a CDS insures the buyer against a default or other negative credit event. In return for this insurance, the seller receives a fee or premium. This is great for the buyer; they can still profit from the MBS and be protected in the event the MBS defaults. The CDS seller is obligated to pay the face value of the MBS in case of a default or other credit event. The CDS seller loves this because he/she knows that the chances of a default are slim so the fee they received for the insurance will be pure profit upon expiration of the insurance contract. Both sides, in a normal market, are solid. The insured can now effectively remove the risk of the MBS off their books and reinvest in more MBS. And once again, buy a CDS to protect from default.

Why do the banks need to remove the risk from their books?

Aside from the obvious reason of capital preservation, Banks have capital requirements which state that they must reserve an X amount of money on the side in the event of loans defaulting or "bank runs" where people withdraw money out of panic. This requirement limits them from betting all their money on investments and risky instruments. By buying insurance on the loans, the loans no longer represents a real risk and thus the bank can do this over and over again without necessarily needing to raise money to fulfill its capital requirements. If the risk is gone, the capital requirement will not need to be increased. The insurance allows the bank to stay below the risk threshold.

But before we go on, there are a few additional details about CDS you should know.

You can buy a CDS without actually owning an MBS or any debt that might be insured by it. You can trade CDS the way you would trade other investment vehicles, although the market is a bit more opaque. For example, you might think that a certain MBS will default; you can buy a CDS against it, even if you don't own the MBS. If it defaults, the CDS Seller is obligated to pay out. Can you see how risky this could be if large default events occurred? Well, that's exactly what happened in this current crisis. Another disturbing fact is that the seller of a CDS is not obligated to have reserves of cash to cover the protection it has sold. This is what was behind the AIG disaster. But before we get into that, let's cover briefly how both sides of a CDS assess their risk.

The name of the kind of risk a CDS poses is called a "Counterparty risk". Each party to the agreement has various risk exposures to one another. There are many risk measures and it would take a separate book to evaluate all potential risks and risk mitigation techniques. But for our purposes, we will discuss basic default risk and who generally assesses the risk involved in a CDS transaction.

Although most firms have in-house risk assessment departments; they often use outside rating agencies like Moody's, Fitch and S&P to evaluate risk on certain debt products, including their own. The thing is, that's part of the problem. The ratings agencies have been called the "high priests" of the market. What they say can make or break companies. Ideally, the rating agencies need to be free of conflict of interest when they do in-depth analysis of credit instruments.

In general, a rating agency is hired to evaluate risk. They use various measures to evaluate the risk profile of any given company, credit instrument or portfolio of credit instruments. The ways in which they assess these risks can often be a bit esoteric and due to this, we will not cover the exact mechanism, but rather, how they contributed to the financial crisis. When they evaluate risk, they assign a rating system that comprises a series of letters. AAA being top credit quality, BBB is riskier, D for default etc. These rating agencies rate everything from individual company debt, to whole countries. Their rating is important because they can often mean the difference between getting good terms on a loan or horrible ones. A company rated AAA will get much better terms than if the company had a BBB rating. Essentially, it's a broad credit score.

As the investment banks created MBS, they needed risk assessment to be done so investors would feel safe when they purchase them. This created a conflict of interest. The investment banks really want to sell these and HIRED the rating agencies. The agencies were not, how shall we say, inclined to give their clients a low rating on their MBS. That's one issue.

The second issue is that they did not have a full understanding of all the mortgages that existed within an MBS and if they did, it was "hush hush". They figured so many are bundled together, the chances of default are slim. But this did not take into account many weaker loans or redundancies in the MBS portfolio. The rating agencies were quick to rate these investment vehicles AAA or close to it. Meaning, they were investment grade in their eyes and thus safe for investors to purchase. This stamp of approval was used by some CDS sellers to assess their own risk. The largest CDS seller of MBS and CDO was AIG. They were so confident in the ratings of the MBS, they wrote CDS on pretty much any MBS they were offered to insure. Every major bank around the world bought insurance with AIG on their MBS portfolios. This insurance, in turn, allowed them to invest in more of them and the cycle continued on. To make matters worse, the bankers and investors used credit to buy MBS thus enhancing return but also increasing risk. And worse still, since one MBS can be sliced up into several different pieces. An insurance company issuing CDS could be insuring against the default of the same loan several times over since it was common for several investors to own pieces of the same MBS and each looking to purchase CDS. This enhanced the risk exposure for the CDS writers. In addition, investment banks were selling MBS and CDS to one another, even further entrenching and binding themselves together. If one went down, others could follow or at least, get seriously wounded.

But now rates were going up, housing prices were going down. Yet the ratings stayed the same for a while. The financial system was just about to unravel. Mortgages were defaulting and CDS were paying face value or defaulting themselves. The banks who borrowed to buy MBS suddenly found their insurance worthless and their debts skyrocketed, they also found the market for these MBS drying up so they couldn't even unload them if they wanted to. This made it difficult to price any of these MBS instruments. If you can't price it, you can't sell it. The bottom was about to drop out from under them. A disaster was unfolding right before their eyes. Banks started to fold and the remaining banks and investment firms refused to lend or do business with one another in fear that the other would default. The credit markets started to freeze up and that's when the trouble really started. In the next chapter we will discuss a few key events in the crisis.

The Music Stopped Playing

Although the panic started to brew early on, especially when Bear Stearns suspended withdrawals in July of 2007, there were earlier signs that something was stirring underneath an unsuspecting market. In February of 2007, HSBC; Europe's largest bank revealed that its US subsidiary, HSBC Finance Corporation had a huge problem with bad mortgage loans so it boosted its loan-loss provision. Meaning, they put more money aside to account for failing mortgages. Eventually they reported a write down of over 11 billion dollars. Around the same time, an index which followed the subprime mortgages indicated that risk was shockingly high. Something was clearly wrong in the subprime lending industry. This became more evident as New Century, a mortgage lender was being slammed in the stock market (They eventually went Bankrupt). The fear and the losses were mounting. The mortgage lenders NovaStar and Kensington; 2 mortgage lenders announced they were curtailing their mortgage lending business. Eventually Kensington had to be bought out. In addition, other mortgage companies like American Home and others either went bankrupt or had to be bought out.

On the housing front; DR Horton, one of the largest builders of new homes in the US warned the market that their upcoming earnings report will reveal huge losses. Not a good sign. But that was only the beginning. The months of August and

September of 2007 saw the crisis spill over into the general market and the general population. BNP Paribas, the French bank started freezing redemptions of their Funds as loan losses mounted. This means they would not allow investors access to their funds. The market became so rattled, the Federal Reserve, as they are want to do, cut interest rates to 5.75%, hoping the added liquidity would help. They also lent an initial 2 billion to the banks to ease the tensions, but it didn't work. HSBC, Lehman Brothers and other companies started to lay off people and shutter mortgage units.

Since Europe had huge exposure to US mortgage markets they too were hit and the European Central Bank (ECB) injected 250 billion Euros into the system to stabilize the general market. That didn't help either. Within a few days a major British bank; Northern Rock had to get bailed out by the Bank of England. The Fed continued to lower rates.

As the 3rd quarter of 2007 arrived it became obvious that the losses incurred by several financial situations were potentially devastating and would be long-lasting.

October started out with Merrill Lynch announcing it had written down $8.4 billion in general mortgages assets and took a loss of $5.5 Billion in subprime mortgages. I was working there at the time and recalled the hushed tones after the losses were announced, it was eerie. This incited panic in the markets and the Fed had to lower rates to 4.5 percent. About a week later, Morgan Stanley announces it has taken a $3.7 billion dollar loss on bad loans. Citigroup, in order to remain afloat had to sell shares to Abu Dhabi to the tune of $7.5 billion dollars. In December, UBS, the Swiss Banking giant revealed $10 billion in write downs. Banks were starting to free as much cash as they could. Bank of America liquidated its $12 billion cash fund as a cushion.

When things couldn't have gotten worse, it did. This prompted the World Bank to inject money into the system, The Fed followed suit and injected an additional $20 billion into the markets. The European Central Bank lent the market an additional 500 Billion Euros over the Christmas Holiday. But nothing was working. To make matters much worse, the Mortgage Insurers were all having their credit ratings cut some from AAA to AA and some to CCC, which is only a few levels away from default. Remember, they also wrote CDS and now had to pay out money they didn't have on defaulting MBS. With all this cash infusion, no one was safe. Merrill Lynch in a desperate effort pleaded for more money and eventually got a $6.2 billion infusion from Tamasek, a Singaporean investment company and Davis Selected advisors. With that, 2007 ended with a horrible thud.

As 2008 rolled in, it was clear it would be much more of the same. Citigroup had to write down $18 billion, UBS confirms and additional $18.4 billion and HSBC confirms an additional $17 billion in losses respectively. As markets continue to collapse, the Fed kept on cutting rates in a desperate attempt to staunch the bleeding, but it didn't work. In a coordinated effort, central banks around the world injected an additional $200 billion into the markets. But yet, nothing.

As the crisis went on unabated, it was starting to wear down the investment banks. Despite outside investments, it was becoming clear that outside investors were not able to help. They had their own problems as well and they were too afraid to make any additional investments. One of Wall Street's oldest firms, Bear Stearns, was in serious trouble and it didn't look like anyone was able to help them. In March of 2008, fearing a catastrophic and systemic collapse of the system, JP Morgan Chase and the Fed worked together to save Bear Stearns from inevitable demise. With the help of the government, JP Morgan purchased Bear for 10 dollars a share; at first they offered only 2 dollars a share. A far cry from its stock price of $133.00 just a few months prior. That may have been the beginning of the end of an historic era on Wall Street, but was only the middle of a much larger crisis. The worst of it was yet to come.

First quarter of 2008 saw more write downs and losses. Germany's Deutsche bank lost $4 billion. Citigroup takes a loss of $15 billion in credit costs etc. Banks raised a record amount of cash through various means to stop the bleeding. Despite this, the banks were all cut by the rating agencies making their lending costs more expensive.

In the late spring of 2008, the proverbial shit, hit the fan. Another Wall Street titan; Lehman Brothers, was showing signs of extreme distress. They posted a $2.8 billion loss and planned to raise $6 billion in new capital through a stock sale. Lehman furthermore sheds some $130 billion in assets to reduce its market risks, but it did nothing for the company. The worst was yet to come. Meanwhile, Countrywide, one the most prolific writers of subprime loans was warding off lawsuits from various states over its lending practices. Countrywide was eventually purchased by Bank of America. But that was nothing compared to what happened to Freddie Mac and Fannie Mae, the government-sponsored mortgage holders, makers and insurers. Their stocks plunge precipitously. All the government needed was for these two mortgage companies to go under. This caused a huge problem for the government. A day after this, the Bank Indymac was seized by government regulators since it was clear they were insolvent. Keep in mind that most bank accounts during this time had only a $100,000 FDIC insurance. This means that the government would insure your deposit for up to $100,000. If you had more than that, you were not guaranteed to get the uninsured portion of your money back. With this in mind, Indymac was being slammed in withdrawals and it was for this reason the government had to take them over. They simply did not have enough money to pay out all those deposits. This would later happen to many banks that year and subsequent years. These were tried and true bank runs, reminiscent of the great depression.

As the summer of hell rolled on, Merrill Lynch declared further write downs to the tune of $5.7 billion. Freddie Mac and Fannie Mae continued to plunge in value. Meanwhile Lehman Brothers was scrambling to find a buyer. At first, Lehman brothers CEO and Chairman Richard Fuld was confident the government would bail them out like they did Bear Stearns, but it appears the government was dragging their feet. As the days went on, several suitors came to buy Lehman brothers, including some US banks as aides to the eventual buyers, but none of them agreed to the terms or were put off by the way the company presented itself. It was clear that the government would not help any buyers in the acquisition of Lehman. They had bigger problems. Not only did they have Freddie Mac and Fannie Mae to worry about. They also learned that AIG, the largest insurer of CDS was about to run out of my money.

On September 9th, 2008, the secretary of the Treasury, Hank Paulson engineered a daring takeover of Freddie Mac and Fannie Mae, he put them in conservatorship. He had to, if he did not, the entire US economy would have collapsed, and countries all over the world would experience such financial shock that many countries could be driven to insolvency. In fact, countries did experience huge financial shocks, some have still not recovered. After the takeover of Freddie Mac and Fannie Mae, it was clear that markets were looking for every reason to fall. With Freddie Mac and Fannie Mae, AIG and Lehman looming large, such a toxic environment made it seem all but hopeless.

Then it happened, on September 15th all hell broke loose. Lehman Brothers declared bankruptcy, the largest at that time. Bank of America bought Merrill Lynch and a day later, the Fed lent AIG $85 billion, which represented an 80% stake in the company in order to allow it to continue to payout on the policies that it insured. If they did not do this, not only would CDS insurance default, it could jeopardize normal insurance policy holders; at least that was what was feared. That would be a catastrophe like none other. Days later, Washington Mutual is seized by the government and sold to JP Morgan chase.

While all this was pretty grim, it got worse. The money market funds all "broke the buck". Money Market funds are accounts that are usually offered by banks and other financial institutions. They are like savings accounts in the sense that they pay interest on deposits. However, unlike savings accounts, these accounts tend to have certain withdrawal restrictions. For example, you may withdraw from it x amount of times a month etc. Another major difference is that the interest earned on the accounts is often derived from investments called "commercial paper". These instruments are very short term debt instruments that companies issue. Some have expirations as short term as 30 days and even fewer days. It's a market that not many people know about. This market helps companies fund their operations on a day to day basis. So, when buying into a money market account, you are essentially buying into these instruments. The accounts are generally guaranteed to have a price of 1 dollar a share. So if you have 500 in that account, you essentially have 500 "shares" of the money market account. Generally speaking, these accounts should never go below $1 per unit. However, when Lehman went under, these money market accounts were worth less than a dollar. Lehman apparently had tons of commercial paper outstanding and now they were close to worthless. This drove much commercial paper to lose value. So in essence, even cash wasn't safe anymore. This was truly a psychologically damaging event. Eventually the US Treasury had to insure them against default.

Investors all over the world started to dump the shares of financial institutions. Many investors decided to sell these companies short. This means that they sold shares in a company before they owned them in hopes of buying them back cheaper. This caused their prices to fall further. Then, in September 17th 2008 the regulatory body to the stock market, The SEC (Securities and Exchange Commission) banned all short selling of financial companies. I guess allowing the markets to dictate where prices needed to be was not good enough. This was a huge blow to the free market ideology everyone so loved and admired.

At this point, investment banks were desperate for money and it looked awful that the government was pumping so much money into them without real government-backed legislation. They eventually urged the investment banks to apply to become bank holding companies. By doing this, it would allow the investment banks to tap into the Federal Reserve System in the event they needed extra cash liquidity to make their capital and other financial requirements. Essentially, they were insured against default in their dealings with one another.

At this time, Citigroup, already a bank holding company was assisted by the government to purchase the banking operations of Wachovia bank. However, Wells Fargo came up with a better deal and eventually purchased Wachovia for $15.1 billion in October of 2008. On November 20th, 2008, the Dow Jones Industrial average hits an 11 1/2 year low and settled at 7552.29. To give you perspective, as of this writing, December 10, 2014, the Dow is currently at 17,801. The blood was running down Wall Street.

During this time, the economy was moving lower and lower, people were being laid-off left and right and home foreclosures were spiked with every month. In 2008 alone, foreclosure filings spiked 81% and 225% since 2006. Unemployment, December of the same year rose to 7.2 percent, almost 3 % higher than the year prior. But these numbers were only going to increase. With outrage spewing from every corner of the globe, it was time for the US government to take decisive action. This piecemeal approach was not working. They had to create real, powerful legislation to protect the financial system.

Troubling Assets

At this point, it was clear that toxic assets aka bad mortgage loans were the big issue here. No one wanted to buy them off the banks and until something was done with them, the banks would continue to get hammered in the market. The market for these toxic assets completely dried up.

Enter TARP

TARP or Troubled Asset Relief Program is a program of the US Government that was meant to purchase the troubled assets of financial firms in order to the strength the overall financial system. Considering nothing else was working, they had to think differently. George W. Bush signed it into law on October 3, 2008.

At first, the TARP program was authorized to spend as much as $700 billion to purchase the troubled assets of various large players in the financial markets. This number, however, was reduced to $475 billion due to the Dodd-Frank Wall Street Reform and Consumer Protect Act. However, Hank Paulson the Secretary of the US Treasury realized that buying troubled assets was just not going to be enough.

Across the pond, United Kingdom's Prime Minister at the time, Gordon Brown found that it was more effective to essentially nationalize British banks by buying shares in them. This gave banks needed capital to survive and by surviving I mean to do what banks are supposed to be doing, lending money. As I stated earlier, the system is based on credit, if credit dries up, the global economy is doomed. Since banks were reluctant to lend to the public as well as to one another, this was a good plan. To use the government's money to mitigate the risk. Of course they banks would need to return the money but the terms were generally good. Hank Paulson eventually decided to do the same for the US Banks. Over time the TARP was honed and made clearer.

To clarify, this was not just a huge handout; the funds being used for TARP had been used for other financial relief for the system:

Including:

1. A program used to buy residential loans from regional banks that had an inordinate supply of them.

2. A methods to create a facility that would insure troubled assets that were purchased under TARP.

3. An MBS bailout fund that would purchase select troubled MBS from the banks.

4. Home ownership preservation: Any loans the government would purchase would seek an opportunity to actually help the homeowner so they won't go into foreclosure.

5. Direct equity purchases of financial firms as discussed above. Essentially "nationalizing" major financial institutions

As part of the "bailout" the financial institutions couldn't just take the money and run. These purchases had some restrictions. One of which was incredibly unpopular amongst bank executives. Mainly, the limits on executive compensation. Some the limitations include the signing of new golden parachutes which allow executives to retire or be terminated while getting a huge payout. This was in addition to the limit on tax deduction the firms can take from these large payouts. Especially troubling was the allowance for salary or payment claw-backs. This means that if the government believes that a payment was excessive, the firm is obligated to try to recover any over-payments from those employees. We aren't talking chump change either.

Here is a breakdown of how much each bank and other financial institutions received as part of the TARP program. The numbers have been rounded to the nearest dollar.

AIG: $40 billion (This is not including earlier bailout money before TARP)

American Express: $3.4 Billion

Bank of America: Two allocations totaling $45 billion

Bank of NY Mellon: $2-3 Billion

Capital One: $3.6 Billion

Citigroup: Two allocations totaling $45 billion

Discover Financial: $1.2 Billion

GMAC Financial aka Ally: $17.3 Billion

Goldman Sachs: $10 Billion

JP Morgan Chase: $25 billion

Morgan Stanley: $10 billion

PNC Financial Services: $7.6 Billion

Regions Financial Corporation: $3.5 Billion

State Street: $2-3 Billion

US Bancorp: $6.6 Billion

Wells Fargo: $25 Billion

It should be noted that most of the financial institutions above have repaid the TARP funds.

Did the program work?

Did the banks use the money to make loans? Not as much as they were expected to. In the end, it was clear banks did not lend as expected but used the money as a way to shore up their own balance sheets, pay down their debts and acquire competitors. Even worse, a lot of the money that was infused into the banking system before TARP was largely used by financial firms to Lobby the government for their own purposes. Regarding the caps in pay, well, that rule was a joke. The firms simply deferred compensation for those individuals. Once TARP was paid, they could simply make those big payouts again. All-in-all I think the market perceived that it worked, but when you drill deeper, the banking sector practices did not change. In fact it got worse, the industry consolidated to the point that there are now only 7 firms controlling the banking system in the United States.

How the Crisis Played Out In the General Economy

We covered, in broad strokes what caused the crisis and how the US government initially tried to control it. Now we will discuss the general impact on the overall economy. Aside from banks falling apart, the real pain was felt in the everyday lives of people weathering the crisis. I will let the numbers speak for themselves.

Unemployment: One of the worst sectors of the economy hit from the crisis was the job market. From October 2006 to April 2007 things were looking pretty good. There was low unemployment, a mere 4.4% on average. However, as the early signs of the crisis were emerging unemployment started to tick up. Not by leaps and bounds, but it was noticeable. It was even more noticeable since from 2003 to April 2007 the rate was dropping and a steady rate. The uptick started to occur in June 2007, the rate increased to 4.6%. Not too bad, but it was in December of 2007 when the rate started to ascended , by December the rate was 5%. It stayed steady at this rate until April of 2008 and then quickly gained speed. From April 2008 to October 2009, the rate of unemployment more than doubled. From 5% to 10.1%. Last time we saw double digit unemployment was in the 1980s. In total, approximately 8.8

million jobs were lost. These numbers are based on government numbers from the Bureau of Labor Statistics. Can these numbers be trusted? I am not 100%; they use many different methods to assess this. But according to research, that includes all measures, the true unemployment rate was double that and still remains high. We must remember that although the unemployment rate as of the time of this writing in December 2014 is 5.8, a good deal of this lower number is due to people completely dropping out of the job market and not necessarily a huge improvement in the job market as a whole. Although it does appear things might be getting better.

Foreclosures: Since the very nature of the economic collapse is due to the real estate market, the rate of people losing their homes to the banks was clearly expected to rise. Based on Realtytrac statistics, from January of 2007 to December of 2011, more than 4 million homes were foreclosed upon that's about 3.4% of total homes with mortgages and at least 8.2 million are in the process. As you can see, the rate of foreclosure may have slowed since the peak of the crisis, but the after effects are still being experienced. The rate might seem low, but in some states, mainly Florida and Nevada the foreclosure filings were much higher. In Florida alone it was 1 in every 33 homes.

Inflation: This measure is another example why the government reported numbers need to be put into question.

Although the rate is an average number, the real affect of inflation has been way beyond the quoted inflation numbers of the US government. Throughout the crisis, the inflation rate hovered between 2.9% to a low of 1% in 11/2010. These numbers should be questioned. It is quite clear that the price of everything has gone up since the crisis began and at a faster rate than 2.9%, far outpacing the reported numbers, some would even say that the number is really twice that amount and slightly more. You may recall, in 2008, grocery giants Walmart and Sams Club rationed flour and rice to customers due to skyrocketing commodity prices. This caused rice prices to double in just a few weeks.

Bread alone rose close to 27% from summer of 2006 to summer of 2008, milk close to 26% for the same period. Eggs and flour close to 55%. Fruits such as apples, Bananas, 29 and 23% respectively. Meats from 4% to 11%. Although the rate appears low on the government reports, it is clearly higher for the average person who lost their jobs during the financial crisis. Prices as of this writing December 2014 are still higher and will remain so.

The Definition of Insanity

"Insanity: Doing the same thing over and over and over again and expecting a different result" - Falsely Attributed to Albert Einstein

As things started to stabilize, the market remained jittery. They got so used to the Federal Reserve's money and didn't want it to stop. They also liked the fact that interest rates are so low. The thing is, the Federal Reserve already lowered interest rates so low they didn't really have room to move lower. The market, however, demanded more. So The Fed continued to add money to the economy via something called quantitative easing in order to satisfy the demand for easy government cash.

Quantitative Easing (QE)

QE is usually used by central banks when other means of stimulating the economy are not enough or have been extended as far as they can go. QE entails the Fed (Other Central banks as well) purchase of specific interest-bearing financial assets from commercial banks and other financial instituions. This supplies more money into the banking system. The financial instruments purchased are generally of longer maturities. When this is done, the price of the financial instruments rise which causes the percentage yield of the asset to go down. (Price and interest yield have an inverse relationship with interest-bearing assets). By buying these assets it keeps the interest rates down, albeit artificially. I find it rather insane that they would keep doing this when it was low interest rates that pretty much got us into this mess. That just goes to show that the Fed really doesn't have many tools to work with... Same ideas concocted in an Ivory Tower.

The Fed instituted 3 QE programs starting in late 2008.

QE 1: In November of 2008 the Federal Reserve kicked off its first QE with the gradual purchase of $600 billion in Mortgage-backed securities, bank debt and treasury notes. Within a little over a year and a half, it accumulated $2.1 Trillion of these assets. As the economy improved, they thought they could put an end to QE1. However, it resumed again in November of 2010.

QE 2: In November 2010 as these instruments matured the holdings went down to about $1.7 trillion by 2012. The Fed, however, wanted to maintain the holdings at about $2.05 trillion which prompted the Fed to buy $30 billion a month of 2 and 10 year Treasury Notes. This would keep short term interest rates down in hopes of spurring on lending.

QE 3: A third round was announced in 13 September 2012. The Federal Reserve decided to buy $40 billion per month, of bonds of various types. During this time, interest rates were close to zero.

In June of 2013 the Fed Chairman at the time, Ben Bernanke announced that the Fed would start to "Taper off" on the QE programs so long as the economic data was improving. When all is said and done and the QE were halted in October of 2014, the Fed accumulated close to $4.5 trillion in assets.

Conclusion

Although the economy seems to be improving and the stock market is up. We must remember that much of the gain in this current market is due to the massive amounts of money that was pumped into the system. In many ways, things have not really changed. As was before the 2008 collapse, the ones who benefited the most from all these financial bailouts were the upper echelons of the population in the US and abroad. In fact, income inequality increased substantially over the period. While banks and corporations were being bailed out. The average person lost their jobs and saw their wages either stagnate or move lower. The party still continues on Wall Street though. The rich are indeed getting richer and the banks are making record profits. They have become so addicted to the easy money that government has thrown at them that it indeed became an addiction. I guess when Ben Bernanke called the resolution of QE as "Tapering". He didn't know how apt that term would become.

It's not over, nothing has changed, what we saw in 2008 will happen again just in a different form. As it states in Ecclesiastes "What was, will be again, there is nothing new under the sun."

About the author

D. M Alon is a bestselling author of 50 books, in 5 different genres and is founder of Numinosity Press Inc.

Before he became an author and teacher, Doron majored in Business and Psychology, spending several years as an entrepreneur, Wall Street Consultant and Healthcare Analyst. During that whole time, he pursued his intellectual and spiritual passions, leading him to the life that he leads today.

Now he writes on a wide variety of topics including History, Self-help, Self-Publishing, and Spirituality.

His conversational writing style and his ability to take complex topics and make them easily accessible has gained him popularity in the genres that he writes for. As he says "Translating esoteric topics and making them easy to understand" is his area of expertise.

Amazon Author Page: www.amazon.com/author/dmalon

ABOUT THE MODERN HISTORIAN SERIES

The goal of the Modern Historian series is to provide concise historical information for people who want to learn more about events and people who were prominent in contemporary history, but do not have the time to read hundreds of pages or purchase expensive study courses. What you read in a Modern Historian Title is the pertinent facts; no filler. Written in an easy to understand and conversational fashion. To learn about future releases in this series please visit THEMODERNHISTORIAN.COM **(coming soon)**

www.ingramcontent.com/pod-product-compliance
Lightning Source LLC
Chambersburg PA
CBHW071937020426
42331CB00010B/2911